IMAGINATIVE INVENTIONS

The Who, What, Where, When, and Why of Roller Skates, Potato Chips, Marbles, and Pie

and More!

by Charise Mericle Harper

Megan Tingley Books

LITTLE, BROWN AND COMPANY
New York Boston

For Papa (French for Dad),
who whistles while he makes things

Little, Brown and Company

Hachette Book Group
1290 Avenue of the Americas, New York, NY 10104
Visit our website at lb-kids.com

Little, Brown and Company is a division of Hachette Book Group, Inc.
The Little, Brown name and logo are trademarks of Hachette Book Group, Inc.

The publisher is not responsible for websites (or their content) that are not owned by the publisher.

First Edition: September 2001

Though all the facts have been verified to the best of the author's ability, it should be noted that creative storytelling and imagination were also used to tell these tales.

The author would like to thank the following for their research information:

Panati's Extraordinary Origins of Everyday Things, by Charles Panati, 1987, Harper & Row; Guinness World Records 2000 Millennium Edition, edited by Nic Kynaston, 2000, Bantam Books; Do Fish Drink Water?: Puzzling and Improbable Questions and Answers, by Bill McLain, 1999, William Morrow and Company; Girls Think of Everything: Stories of Ingenious Inventions by Women, by Catherine Thimmesh, 2000, Houghton Mifflin Company; www.designershoes.com/about_footwear.htm (a site about shoes); www.nabisco.com (animal cookies); web.mit.edu/invent/index.html (a great site about inventors); www.wrigley.com (about gum); www.hometown.aol.com/rkaczur/history.htm (history of gum); www.nacgm.org/consumer/funfacts.html (fun facts about gum); home.nycap.rr.com/useless/ (a great site about useless information); www.elliskaiser.com/doughnuts (about doughnuts); www.rollerskatingmuseum.com (facts about roller skating); www.blocksite.com/reference/faq.htm#history (about marbles); www.earthdaybags.org (site devoted to the Earth Day Project); www.wham-o.com (Frisbee site); www.piecouncil.org (about pie)

Library of Congress Cataloging-in-Publication Data

Harper, Charise Mericle.
Imaginative inventions : the who, what, where, when, and why of roller skates, potato chips, marbles, and pie (and more!) / by Charise Mericle Harper. — 1st ed.
p. cm.
ISBN 978-0-316-34725-9
1. Inventions — History — Juvenile literature. [1. Inventions — History.] I. Title.
T15.H344 2001
609 — dc21
00-062443

17 18 19 20

IM

Printed in China

The illustrations for this book were created on chipboard using acrylic paint, wire, pencil, and collage.
The text was set in Birdlegs, and the display type was handlettered by the artist.

How are inventions made?
Is it really hard to do?
To think of something people need
that's different and brand-new?

CONTENTS

POTATO CHIPS

too thick

In Saratoga Springs
in 1853
the first chip was invented
very accidentally.

Now the cook, whose name was George,
had never been to France.
He said, "I'd love to travel
but I've never had the chance."

One day there was a customer.
Let's say his name was Rick.
He ordered some of George's fries
then said, "These are too thick!"

Now Rick had been to France —
he said, "French fries should be thinner
I'll just wait until you fix these,
then I'll finish up my dinner."

CHEF

FR France

"France, France, fancy pants!"
Chef George was not impressed.
He cut Rick's fries up super thin
for being such a pest.

PEST

just right

Well, Rick said, "My friend George,
I like these more than fries.
They're crispy and they're crunchy —
you deserve a cooking prize."

The ridged chip
was invented in 1983.
It is the king of
dipping chips.

Americans eat the
most chips on
Super Bowl Sunday:
11.3 million pounds.

Most popular flavors:
U.S.: barbecue
Canada: ketchup, vinegar
Greece: oregano
other country.

People in the U.S. eat
more potato chips
than people in any

Who: George Crum
Where: Saratoga
Springs, New York
When: 1853

FACTS

FRISBEE®

In 1957
flying saucers were his passion.
Walter dreamed of men from space
and what they'd wear as fashion.

UNIDENTIFIED
FLYING
OBJECT

He made a little disc of tin
and threw it in the air.
And from far away it looked as if
a UFO was there.

He thought he was the first
to think of such a game.
But others had invented it
and given it a name.

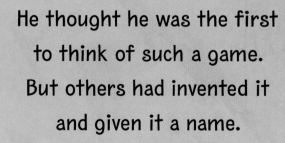

Students at a school called Yale
would eat a Frisbie Pie,
then they'd throw the empty tin
high across the campus sky.

SCHOOL

Walter heard of the Frisbie tins and said,
"That name is great!"
So he called his toy a Frisbee
then ate pie to celebrate.

Who: Walter Frederick Morrison
Where: California
When: around 1957

The longest distance a Frisbee flying disc has been thrown is 693.3 feet.

More Frisbees are sold every year than footballs, baseballs, and basketballs combined.

There is a special Frisbee made just for dog competitions.

Frisbee is a registered trademark owned by Wham-O, Inc.

7

FACTS

PIE

GREEK FLAG

In Greece there was a baker
1,600 years ago
who said, "I'll make a stew,
and then cover it with dough."

It's said the world's first pie
was probably made of meat
and it wasn't until later
that a pie became a sweet.

PIG

GOAT

CHICKEN

BLUEBERRY

CHERRY

BANANA

Today we have so many kinds
like pumpkin, lime, or cherry.
Your favorite flavor — is it peach?
Or rhubarb with strawberry?

CHOCOLATE

STRAWBERRY

LEMON

APPLE

LIME

PEACH

PECAN

PEAR

MPKIN

Who: unknown
Where: Greece
When: 5th century

Apple is the most popular flavor in North America, except at Thanksgiving, when the most popular flavor is pumpkin.

The state of Illinois produces the most pumpkins for pumpkin pie.

The largest pecan pie ever made was 40 feet in diameter.

Cream pies are the pie of choice for throwing.

FACTS

PIGGY BANK

In the Middle Ages
pots were made from pygg.
It was an orange clay
that wasn't hard to dig.

When someone had some money
to save or hide away,
they kept it in their pygg jar
for a future rainy day.

Some potter probably said, after giving it some thought, "What if I take my fine pygg clay and make a pig-shaped pot?"

5¢
+ 5¢
10¢

Well, soon the other potters who formed and shaped the clay were making jars in piggy shapes just like they do today.

FACTS

Who: unknown   Where: England
When: pygg used to make pots,
Middle Ages; first pig-shaped
pot created in 18th century

If you saved one penny for every day you were alive, you'd have:

1 year old — $3.65
2 years old — $7.30
3 years old — $10.95
4 years old — $14.60
5 years old — $18.25
6 years old — $21.90
7 years old — $25.55
8 years old — $29.20

The largest piggy bank collection has 4,175 pigs in it.

EYEGLASSES

Silvano couldn't see that well,
although he wasn't blind.
He had a lot of trouble
finding things not hard to find.

He lost his pants, his socks, his shirt—
he even lost his dog.
He said, "I've got to fix my eyes
and clear away this fog."

One day in the year 1280
while drinking from a glass,
he was looking through the bottom
when he said, "I see at last."

So he made two discs of finest glass.
He made them thick and round.
He held them right up to his eyes
and this is what he found.

"My pants, my socks, my shirt!" he cried.
His heart was filled with glee,
and there right by his favorite chair,
his dog scratching a flea.

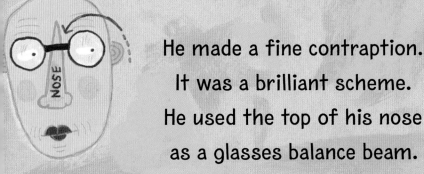

He made a fine contraption.
It was a brilliant scheme.
He used the top of his nose
as a glasses balance beam.

The first glasses were much heavier and often caused headaches or sore noses if worn for too long.

Arms for glasses to fit over your ears were invented 400 years after glasses. Until then people tried to balance the glasses on their nose or used leather straps to tie them to their head.

Seventy percent of all people in the U.S. wear glasses or contact lenses.

Who: thought to be Silvano Armato
Where: Pisa, Italy
When: 1280s

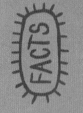
FACTS

13

DOUGHNUT

The doughnut was invented
500 years ago.
The first ones didn't have a hole
and were just balls of dough.

The Pilgrims loved the doughnut
and they brought the recipe
from Holland to America
in boats across the sea.

There was a captain of a boat
who said, "I don't know why
doughnuts can't be bigger,
I'll just ask my mom to try."

He poked holes in the middle
so they'd cook more evenly,
then his mom cooked up the doughnuts
which they both ate happily.

Around 2 billion dollars worth of doughnuts are sold every year in the United States.

The most popular doughnut with kids is the chocolate frosted.

Midwest and West Coast people seem to prefer raised doughnuts while East Coast people seem to like cake-style doughnuts best.

Who: Hanson Gregory was the first to poke a hole in a doughnut.
Where: Rockport, Maine
When: 1847

FACTS

FLAT-BOTTOMED PAPER BAG

The flat-bottomed paper bag
long ago was hard to make,
and some said, "Not quite worth
all the trouble it would take."

Workers first would fold the bags
and then they'd add the glue.
This made the bags expensive,
plus it took too long to do.

Margaret was a lady
working in the factory.
She said, "Here's an idea
that could help this company."

"Wouldn't it be faster
if machines could make these bags?
I bet I could invent one
without too many snags."

In the year of 1870
her machine was finally done.
And today we use her bags
for groceries, lunch, and fun.

PAPER

PAPER
BAG

WORKER

COOKIES
APPLE
EGGS
MILK

COOKIE
SANDWICH
BANANA

Who: Margaret E. Knight
Where: Massachusetts
When: 1870

America's super-
markets purchase
25 billion paper
bags a year.

For the Earth Day Groceries Project, students paint grocery bags with Earth Day themes and return them to the store. The bags are then distributed to shoppers on Earth Day (April 22). In 1999, 1,135 schools participated and painted 374,472 bags.

FACTS

HIGH-HEELED SHOES

There was a short French king
in the sixteenth century
who said, "I must be taller.
It's just what I want to be!"

Now his subjects, they were loyal,
so they said, "What should we do?"
Said a timid little cobbler,
"I could build a higher shoe."

The king said, "These are great!"
and he marched around the court.
He was taller than before
and no longer feeling short.

But it happened all too fast,
for poor Louis the short king —
by wearing high-heeled shoes,
he'd begun a fashion thing.

Now with everyone in heels
he no longer seemed that tall,
so he had some new shoes made
that would tower over all.

It was then that he got angry
and he made a big decree,
saying, "No more high heels on a man!
Unless that man is me!"

Who: unknown
Where: France
When: 16th century

Today there is still a heel style
called the Louis heel after the
king, but most high-heeled
shoes are worn by women.

The first shoes ever
made were sandals to
protect the feet from
rocks and sharp sticks.

Until 1850 there were no
left shoes or right shoes
—both shoes were made
exactly the same.

FACTS

WHEELBARROW

Back in the year 200,
in China far away,
lived a man who carried things
most each and every day.

Mr. Liang was his name
and his arms were very strong,
but he worried that the carrying
would stretch them out too long.

He carried for the army.
He carried for his wife.
He was a man who moved things,
transportation was his life.

One day while on a narrow path
he said, "That's it, I'm through!
There's got to be a better way
to do the things I do."

He thought all through his dinner.
He thought while in his bed.
When he woke up he was smiling
because the plan was in his head.

He sawed and banged all morning
and by lunchtime he was done.
He'd made a handy wheelbarrow,
and it was the world's first one.

CHOPSTICKS

GOLDFISH

FIREWORKS

FACTS

Who: Chuko Liang
Where: China
When: A.D. 200

Wheelbarrows are still widely used in rural China to transport almost everything.

Today contractors building high-rises or houses use wheelbarrows the most.

People also use wheelbarrows in their gardens to transport dirt and flowers from place to place.

CHEWING GUM

There was a famous general
who came from Mexico.
His name was Santa Anna
and he won the Alamo.

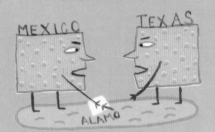

SAP

He moved to Staten Island,
1860 was the year,
and he loved to chew a gummy sap
that he said had no peer.

One day he met a man
who said, "Gee, that sap is neat.
I'll change it into rubber,
it will be an easy feat."

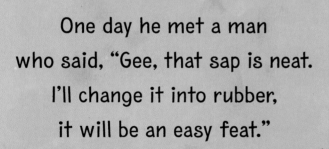

Even though he tried his best,
the inventor had no luck,
and he wondered what to do
with all the sap left in his truck.

He thought of Santa Anna
and of how he liked to chew.
So he said, "There must be others
who would like to do it too."

His Adams New York Gum
sold in 1871,
and it only cost a penny
and was loved by everyone.

Who: Thomas Adams
Where: Hoboken,
New Jersey
When: 1871

Bubble gum is pink because
it is the only color dye the
inventor had when he was
making it.

The most popular
flavors are pepper-
mint, spearmint, and
cinnamon.

The largest bubble
ever blown was 23
inches in diameter.

North American kids
spend approximately
half a billion dollars
a year on gum.

FACTS

ROLLER SKATES

Joseph lived in Belgium
in 1759.
He loved to play his violin
and practiced all the time.

There was to be a party,
a fancy fun affair.
Joseph said, "I'll make an entrance,
so my friends will know I'm there."

Since the party was on land,
he knew ice skates wouldn't do,
so he took his favorite footwear
and put wheels under each shoe.

The night of the big party,
with wheeled skates upon his feet,
Joseph glided in while playing
and the crowd said, "Oh, how sweet."

But he hadn't practiced stopping
so he crashed into a wall,
and his violin was broken
'cause he'd smashed it in the fall.

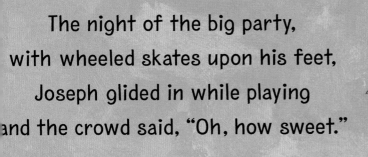

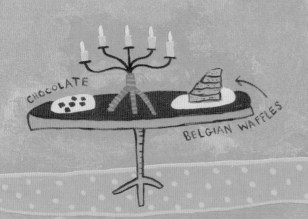

CHOCOLATE

BELGIAN WAFFLES

So this time it ended badly
but he didn't shed a tear.
He said, "I'll just have to practice
and then try again next year."

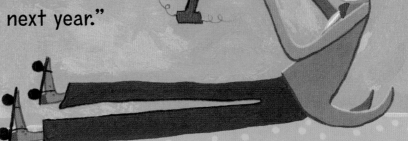

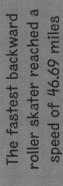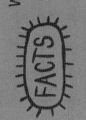

SCARAB

MARBLES

There is a game that has been played
5,000 years or more.
It started back in Egypt
rolling stones across the floor.

STONES

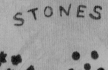
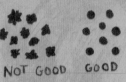

NOT GOOD   GOOD

CAMEL

The stones were smooth and shiny,
and colorful and round,
and the children each took turns
rolling them across the ground.

RED SEA

PYRAMID

SMOOTH

GRASS

---- CAT'S EYE

CAIRO

Children play it still today
with round balls made of glass.
In school yards and on sidewalks
(but never on the grass).

Marbles are sometimes used to move heavy crates by rolling the box over a marble pad.

Marble sizes range from 1/2 inch in diameter to 2 1/2 inches in diameter.

The most common marble is called the cat's eye, a clear marble with a colored four-leaf clover inside.

Recently a marble sold for $15,000.

Who: unknown
Where: Egypt
When: 3000 B.C.

FACTS

VACUUM CLEANER

Cecil was a man
who said, "I like things clean!
But I don't want to work too hard,
so I'll make a machine."

He did some strange experiments
and tried to suck up dirt,
from pillows and on furniture
until his lips were hurt.

MINI BROOM

DUSTPAN

FEATHER DUSTER

And then he tried some blowing,
but said, "No, that seems wrong!
I think I need a wind machine
that sucks up dirt real strong."

DIRTY

CLEAN

1901 was the year
that he built his first machine.
It took two men to operate
but really got things clean.

THEN

NOW

Who: H. Cecil Booth
Where: England
When: 1901

Before 1940 most vacuums were sold door-to-door. A salesman would knock on your door and ask if you would like a demonstration, and then he would come in and drop dirt on your carpet so you could see how well his vacuum could pick it up.

The first vacuum cleaner was as large as a refrigerator and took two men to operate — one to push it on its wheel and one to operate its hose.

FACTS

29

ANIMAL COOKIES

It happened back in England
over 100 years ago.
A cook said, "Let's make animals,
with all this cookie dough."

Then someone in America
said, "That's a great idea!
We'll do it, too, with a bigger zoo,
and sell those cookies here!"

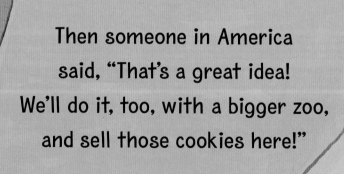

SEAL

They made eighteen new animals
and put them in a box.
A bear, a seal, and monkeys, too,
but not a pig or fox.

LION

GIRAFFE

BEAR

GORILLA

MONKEY

So you can bite a zebra's ear,
or chew on a giraffe,
or even nibble elephant toes
until they make you laugh.

Who: unknown
Where: England
When: 1890

Who: Nabisco
Where: U.S.
When: 1902

The first animal cookies made in the U.S. were made by Nabisco. They were called Barnum's Animals, after the famous circus.

Other animal cookies include: bison, camel, cougar, hippopotamus, hyena, kangaroo, rhinoceros, sheep, tiger, and zebra.

FACTS

31

A LAST WORD ABOUT INVENTIONS

Some inventions solve a problem,
like glasses to help you see.
Then there are others just for fun,
like skates or the Frisbee.

Inventions can be lucky,
like the great potato chip,
or even come from other lands,
like doughnuts on a ship.

Inventors can be young
or as old as ninety-three,
they just need imagination
to see things creatively.

ALPHABET
BLOCKS
FOR THE
BLIND
(INVENTED 1996)

KRYSTAL: 11-YEAR-OLD GIRL INVENTOR